By Laura Williams
Translated By Lee Ji-su

자다

[jada] - to sleep

목욕하다

[mog-yoghada] - to take a bath

기다

[gida] - to crawl

놀다

[nolda] - to play

앉다

[anjda] – to sit

울다

[ulda] – to cry

서서

[seoseo] - to stand

박수 치다

[bagsu chida] - to clap

읽다

[ilgda] - to read

먹다

[meogda] - to eat

마시다

[masida] - to drink

웃다

[usda] - to laugh

껴안다

[kkyeoanda] - to hug

걷다

[geodda] – to walk

달리다

[dallida] - to run

키스하다

[kiseuhada] - to kiss

점프하다

[jeompeuhada] – to jump

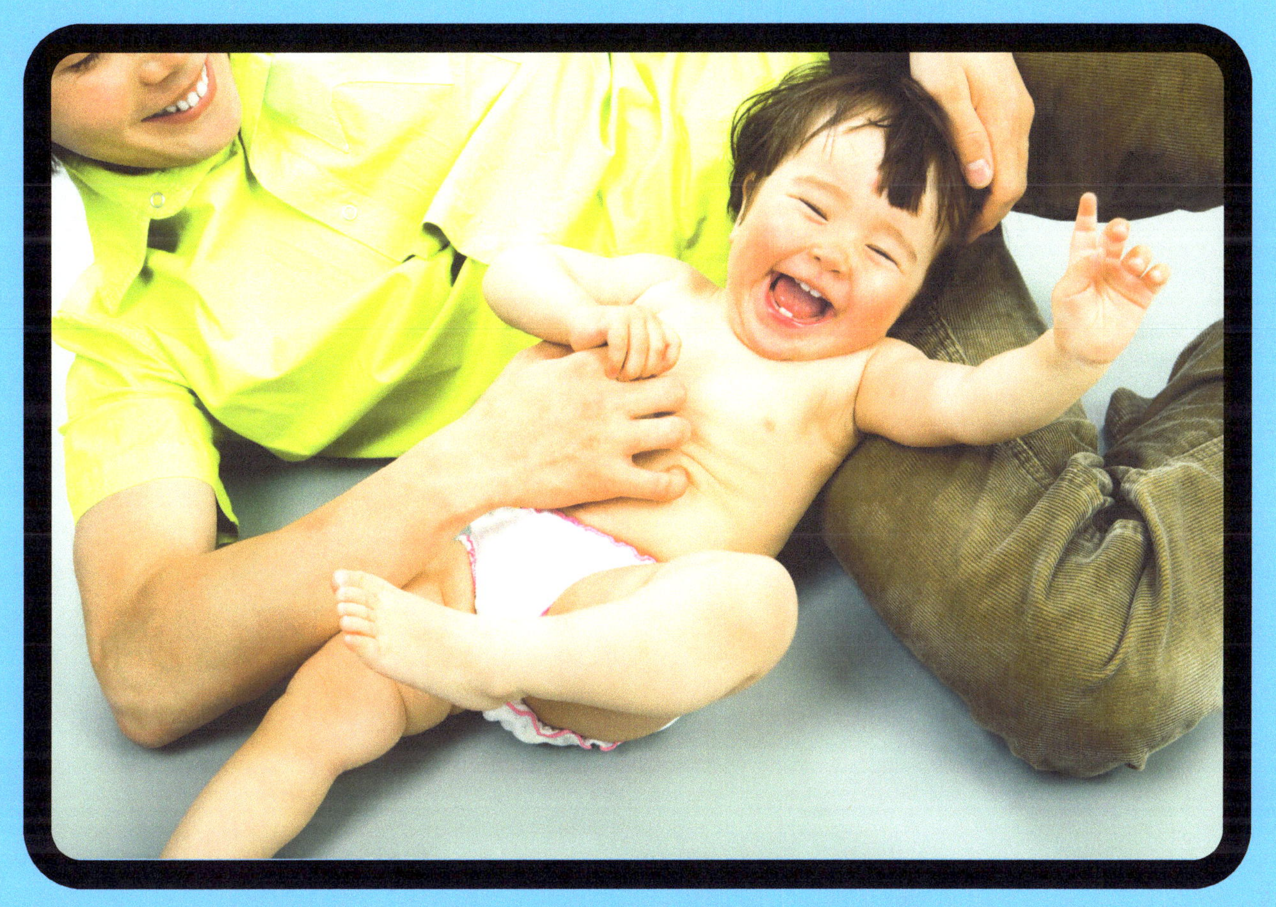

간지럽히다

[ganjileobhida] - to tickle

춤을 추다

[chum-eul chuda] - to dance

요리하다

[yolihada] – to cook

무릎을 꿇다

[muleup-eul kkulhda] - to kneel

밀다

[milda] - to push

당기다

[dang-gida] - to pull

쓰다

[sseuda] - to write

노래하다

[nolaehada] - to sing

In the same collection

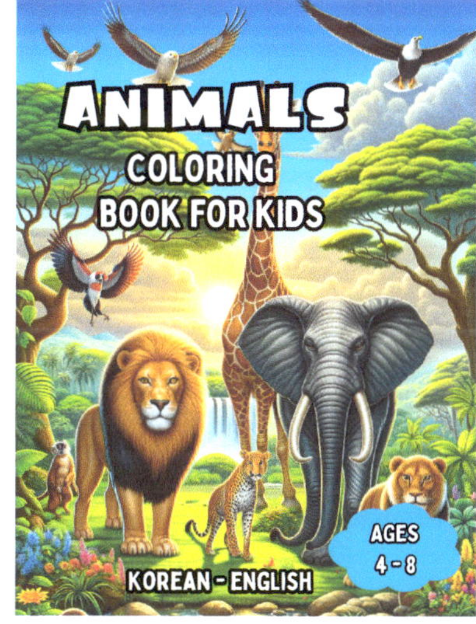

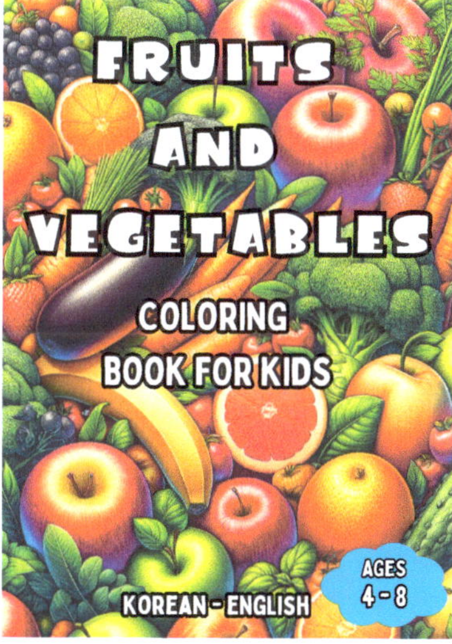